CONTENTS

Cover: Claude
Monet, *Water
Lilies, Evening Effects*,
1897-98,
oil on canvas,
73 x 100 cm
(detail).

Pages 2-3 and 66-67:
Claude Monet
with the duc
de Trévise, in his
second studio
at Giverny, 1920.
© Roger-Viollet.

Above:
Claude Monet
(1840-1926),
Waterloo Bridge,
c. 1900,
pastel, 30 x 47 cm.

PREFACE

by M. Bernard Zehrfuss,
Perpetual Secretary of the Académie des Beaux-Arts

At the edge of a quiet street in the fashionable Muette neighborhood near the Bois de Boulogne, far from the noises of the city, a visitor can discover a surprising Empire-style mansion surrounded by more recent architectural styles. This former hunting lodge was constructed by maréchal Kellermann when Paris was still very close to the countryside. It was purchased in 1882 by Jules Marmottan, who felt that this residence was the ideal setting for his private collections, which were essentially devoted to the Napoleonic era. This passion for the history of one man and one era was shared by his son Paul, who filled his offices in Boulogne with a large number of documents and works of art concerning the imperial period; this became the Marmottan library. In 1932, Paul Marmottan bequeathed his two mansions and their contents to the Académie des Beaux-Arts, which two years later gave Paris a new museum on the rue de Boilly, framed by parks and gardens on all sides: the Ranelagh square, the Bois de Boulogne and the charming garden facing the sitting rooms of the mansion.

In keeping with the spirit of such a generous donor, the Académie first exhibited the Empire collections. Yet after receiving a series of bequests, the museum became more diversified and offered a wider view of the nineteenth century. Today, visitors can explore this prestigious decor that contains objects made of gold, marble and precious hardwoods, as well as superb Impressionist paintings by Monet and his friends and, in a separate room, more than 300 medieval illuminations. The Marmottan Museum is a special place that has attracted and continues to attract art lovers. Indeed, visitors are not the only ones to appreciate this private space; many donors have contributed works, including Victorine de Bellio, the daughter of Monet's personal doctor, who added a new dimension with the bequest of a collection of some of the most famous Impressionist works; Michel Monet, the master's youngest son, who also donated close to 100 works; and of course Monet, Pissarro, Morisot, Renoir and Caillebotte. Daniel Wildenstein expanded the artistic horizons of the museum by donating all of the illuminated pages collected by his father. And finally, Nelly Sergeant-Duhem, who added to the existing collection with a bequest that included a work by Boudin, an artist who greatly influenced the magical "gardener" of Giverny. In addition to these extraordinary donations, other donors from abroad expanded the collections of this "hunting lodge": American Lila Acheson-Wallace, and others collectors from Asia – Huang from Taiwan and Kobayashi from Japan – all admirers who took it upon themselves to help rejuvenate the museum.

On behalf of the Académie, my colleague Arnaud d'Hauterives, curator of the museum, and myself, I would like to honor their memory and express our deepest gratitude. I would now like to invite the reader to follow in their footsteps through these rooms that contain so many special memories. You will be greeted by the *Water Lilies*, and above all, by *Impression: Sunrise*.

Left to right:
Empire furniture:
armchairs and chairs
in front of a
flat mahogany desk
by Pierre-Antoine
Bellangé.
Photograph: G. Fessy.

Portraits of Jules
(1829-83) and
Paul Marmottan
(1856-1932).
© Bibliothèque
Marmottan.

Jules and Paul
Marmottan: Collectors

The Marmottan Museum stands in the heart of the Ranelagh gardens, in a triangle of greenery in the lovely Muette neighborhood. The bright chandeliers are just visible through the high windows of the mansion, which still looks like a private residence. Indeed, the former owners are in a place of honor just inside the door: a bust of Jules Marmottan faces another one of his son Paul. Under the sculpture of the latter is an inscription in marble: "Because I was told that all of my collections deserve to be kept forever for the instruction of everyone, I bequeath them, as well as my mansion, to the Institut de France for the Académie des Beaux-Arts." This was the birth of the museum, created by two generations of art collectors whose temperaments and aims complemented each other. Originally from the Savoy region, the Marmottan family moved to northern France during the reign

Marmottan was an exemplary figure among the bankers of the Industrial Revolution and he was often solicited for advice. He remained mayor of Bruay after 1879, when he was appointed by the government to be chief treasurer and paymaster for the Gironde region. He also worked as an administrator for many companies, including the Lille-Béthune railway line, the coal mines of Ferfay (Pas-de-Calais), the Compagnie immobilière de Paris and the Compagnie générale transatlantique. As his primary concern was to efficiently distribute coal, he actively promoted the Canal du Nord between Lens and Paris.

of Louis XV. The passion for art in this dynasty may have begun with Pierre Marmottan, born in 1780, the son of a pharmacist. An amateur draftsman, Pierre Marmottan twice won awards from the Académie de Valenciennes – in 1799 and again in 1805 – but despite this encouragement, he did not pursue his artistic studies, preferring instead to work in the more sensible field of banking. His son Jules, born in 1829, received a traditional education: after finishing *collège* in Valenciennes, he studied law at the university in Paris and started working with a stockbroker named Mahou. One year later he became a leading partner in Edmond Dollfus' business. The year 1862 was a turning point in his career: he became director of the Bruay coal mining company in the Pas-de-Calais. The situation of the young company at the time was serious: it was heavily in debt and had just lost a costly court case, and only one of the coal pits, the first, was productive. Jules Marmottan courageously devoted all his intelligence and talents to this company. His efforts paid off: within a few years the business expanded and became remarkably successful. The town, which grew from 700 to 6,000 inhabitants in just 20 years, owed a great deal to this benefactor, who also became mayor of Bruay in 1870. Schools, local roads, public baths, relief funds and medical services for workers were created under his leadership. Jules

In 1882, one year before he died, Jules Marmottan acquired the mansion facing the Ranelagh gardens. This enclave of greenery was earlier famous for the ball (for which admission was charged) created in 1774 "on the initiative of Lord Ranelagh in London." Even then it was well known as a calm and tranquil park. The mansion was purchased from the heirs of François Kellermann, a maréchal of France who became duc de Valmy in 1808 in recognition of his famous victory. Paul selected a neo-classical design for the office-library, in keeping with his fondness for the Empire style. The sitting rooms and galleries of the future museum perfectly reflect the nineteenth-century spirit; here, like at Chantilly, the furniture, objects and paintings are crowed close together throughout the mansion.

Left to right and
top to bottom:
Paul Marmottan in
his office in 1911.
© Bibliothèque
Marmottan.

Overall view of
the gallery at the
turn of this century.
© Bibliothèque
Marmottan.

The Marmottan
mansion before
the construction of
the side wings.
© Archives
du musée Marmottan.

The Marmottan
Museum today,
viewed
from the garden.

Below: Adrienne-
Marie-Louise
Grandpierre-Deverzy
(active between
1822 and 1855),
*The Studio
of Abel de Pujol*,
1822,
oil on canvas,
96 x 129 cm.

Right, top to bottom:
Etienne Bouhot (1780-
1862), *The Courtyard
of the Institut
de France*, undated,
oil on canvas,
38 x 46 cm.

Louis-Philibert
Debucourt (1755-
1832), *View of
the Arc de Triomphe
and the Grande
Finale of
the Fireworks Display*,
1810, etching
and watercolor,
26 x 37 cm.

On his death in 1883 he left a considerable fortune to his son Paul, as well as a mansion located opposite the Ranelagh gardens he had purchased in 1882 from the Kellermann heirs, and a large collection of artwork. Throughout his entire life, Jules was a well-informed, yet discreet, client of various antique dealers, although he mostly purchased work from Antoine Brasseur, a dealer and art restorer from Lille who worked in Cologne from 1847 to 1887. He accumulated a collection of German, Flemish and Italian primitives. The Haute-Epoque furniture, fifteenth-century wood sculptures and Renaissance tapestries are also in keeping with the austere personality of the collector.

Paul was very different from his father, despite his inherited "passion for order and sense of grandeur." Born in 1856, Paul studied at the Collège de Juilly where he obtained – in reminiscence of his paternal grandfather – the first prize in drawing in 1867. At the age of 18 he decided to travel: he went to Italy of course, but also to Egypt where he followed in the footsteps of Auguste Mariette, "the eminent antique dealer." By the time he turned 21, he had published his first collection of poems, *Les Primevères*, and was a regular contributor to the *Bulletin administratif, commercial, artistique et littéraire du XVIe arrondissement*, also known as *Paris-Passy*. Nevertheless, under pressure from his father, Paul obtained his law diploma and started working, reluctantly, as an advisor in the prefecture at Evreux in 1882. He admitted that he was "much more interested in the delicate tastes of the artist, the collector and the man of letters than in the troubled areas of politics or the narrow world of the functionary." He did not have to endure this job for long; on the death of his father one year later, he gained his freedom and was able to devote himself fully to his passions: travel and historical and artistic research. He went to Belgium, Holland, the banks of the Rhine, Poland, Spain and Switzerland.

One of the most note-
worthy characteristics
of Paul Marmottan is
that he was interested in
the Napoleonic era at a
time when others preferred to ignore or even
despise it. In his journeys, he was able to ac-
cumulate a vast amount of documentation on
the subject, works that were added to his considerable library concerning the Empire, including :
le Général Fromentin et l'armée du Nord, *le
Royaume d'Etrurie*, *Bonaparte et la république de
Lucques*, *les Troupes de Joseph Napoléon en Es-
pagne*, *Elisa Bonaparte*, *les Arts en Toscane sous
Napoléon*, *le Style Empire* and so on. Over the
years, he became an expert on art created during
the Empire and the Consulate in Paris (and
wrote several studies, including *les Statues de
Paris* and *le Pont d'Iéna*). This immense library
was kept in his home in Boulogne, purchased
in 1921; it included thousands of volumes
concerning the years from 1799 to 1814. Paul

Above, left to
right, top to bottom:
Empire cups
and saucers,
*Woman Giving a
Drink to a Soldier*
and *Venus and
Cupid*, undated.

Above: Small round
sitting room
facing the garden;
to the left, the
geographical clock
commissioned
by Napoleon I
Photograph: G. Fessy.

THE EMPIRE FASHION

Under the influence of Brongniart, appointed to direct the Manufacture de Sèvres in 1800, the production of French porcelain recovered after a period of total decline. Paul Marmottan was particularly fond of Dagoty's designs and purchased a beautiful collection of cups decorated with antique images. The most surprising object, however, is unquestionably the "geographical clock" designed in 1813 in honor of Napoleon I. It was modified during the Restoration and acquired by Louis XVIII, who then gave it to the duchesse de Berry. Napoleon's head was replaced by profiles of Apollo and Diana; and images depicting different time zones decorate the face of the clock, instead of the original design of "twelve subjects in the history of the Emperor."

Top to bottom:
Dagoty, Empire cup and saucer with mythological design, 1804, porcelain, Manufacture de l'Impératrice.

Detail of the face of the geographical clock, 1813-21: twelve painted miniature medallions on porcelain

portray noon in various parts of the world, Manufacture de Sèvres, 2.28 meters high.

Marmottan is an unusual scholar in that it is difficult to separate the historian from the collector. "I arrived at Napoleonic history through art," he said. As opposed to his father, he did not rely on just one dealer, preferring – as he wrote in his book concerning the French school of painting (*l'Ecole française de peinture, 1780-1840*) – to collect his artwork in a more clever way: "When one has acquired an artistic judgment through a combination of personal taste and conscientious study of the old schools, it is not necessary to frequent the large public sales … It is still possible to find paintings from the French school before 1830 in certain small

sales after a death and from certain dealers in curios (who are generally extremely ignorant). In this case, all it takes is a bit of skill to purchase a valuable painting for a low price."
Hector Lefuel, a close friend of Paul Marmottan and first curator of the museum, wrote an introduction to the first catalogue of the collection. In it, he discussed the pride of Paul Marmottan, who "liked to recall the origin of a great number of his works of art made for Napoleon or for the imperial family. Up until the end, he wanted to acquire – to 'save' as he said – the memories of a past for which he felt nostalgia and respect." This passion often meant that he selected the

works on the basis of their historical value only, as reflected in the many anonymous views (*A Parisian Street in the Nineteenth Century, The Stables of the Duc d'Angoulême, The Villa de Pline on Lake Como* and so on), or their esthetic interest, such as the surprising eagle clock/vase, which is similar to a piece in the Queen of England's collection. Many well-known artists (Boilly, Kinson, Lefebvre, Bartolini, Prud'hon and Robert) are also included in this unique collection that Paul Marmottan, who died childless in 1932, chose to bequeath to the Institut de France;

in this, he may have been inspired by the gesture of Nelly Jacquemart-André 20 years earlier. The Boulogne library and the museum both carry his name, ensuring his posterity; yet he also left a considerable amount of money to Malmaison, the Army Museum, Versailles, Carnavalet, Sèvres, the Costume Museum and the Decorative Arts Museum, as well as to many other museums throughout France. He also left 15 million francs to the Assistance Publique, which added another dimension to this great scholar: that of a true philanthropist. **Laure Murat**

Left to right:
Auguste Renoir
(1841-1919),
*Claude Monet
Reading*, 1872,
oil on canvas,
61 x 50 cm.

Claude Monet
(1840-1926),
*On the Beach
at Trouville*,
1870-71,
oil on canvas,
38 x 46 cm.

The Impressionist Collection

by Sophie Monneret

Donations transformed the Museum – which was originally devoted to Napoleonic history – into a sanctuary of Impressionism. Three bequests to the Académie des Beaux-Arts mark this transformation: one from Victorine Donop de Monchy (Dr. de Bellio's daughter) in 1957; another from Michel Monet (the artist's son) in 1966; and finally, a third from Nelly Sergeant-Duhem (adopted daughter of the painter Duhem) in 1985.

Only part of Dr. de Bellio's collections went to the Marmottan Museum, but the works are superb and include *Impression: Sunrise*, the seminal painting of Impressionism. "Whenever one of us urgently needed money," recalled Renoir, "he ran to the Riche café, where he was sure to find M. Bellio." This Romanian aristocrat came to France during the Second Empire. He practiced medicine only for his friends and collected art with a generous passion. It may have been one of his relatives, Georges Bibesco, for whom Renoir worked in 1869, who kindled Bellio's interest in what was considered to be controversial painting at the time. From Monet in 1874 to Gauguin in 1891, his purchases follow the evolution of Impressionism; the paintings in this collection represent the very essence of the movement. The gift from Michel Monet protrays a discontinuous itinerary through his father's life: portraits (his first wife, his two sons), works by such friends as Jongkind, Renoir and Caillebotte (purchased or gifts) and works from his travels (Riviera, Norway and Holland). The large studies of the Giverny garden complete the excellent collection. They illustrate the creative process in its pure state, at the magical moment when the impression appeared: was it expressionism? or abstraction?

The collection of Duhem and his wife begins with Boudin and continues through the poetic and intimate work of their friend Le Sidaner. Impressionist works, represented in both the virulence of Guillaumin and discretion of Lebourg, hang alongside Symbolist paintings by Carrière. An admirable still-life by Gauguin adds an accent of exoticism to the ensemble.

This immensely famous painting has been mocked, showered with praise and even stolen, but it has always fascinated art lovers. First exhibited during a group show organized in 1874 in Nadar's studio by Monet and his friends, this painting gave its name to the movement that began with this exhibition. Monet, asked to give a title to the work by the editor of the catalogue (Edmond Renoir), suggested "Impression." Renoir added "Sunrise." The satirical newspaper *Charivari* mockingly baptized the style "Impressionism." The canvas (which may have been antedated by Monet), depicts the old harbor of Le Havre seen from the Amirauté Hotel. This painting – a synthesis of watercolors by Turner and Jongkind, as well as the Japanese prints and Chinese ink drawings Money saw in London and Holland – is amazingly modern. First purchased in May of 1874 by Ernest Hoschedé, it was acquired by Dr. de Bellio during a court-ordered sale in 1878.

IN THE COUNTRYSIDE

Below, top to bottom:
Claude Monet,
Field of Yellow Irises
at Giverny, 1887,
oil on canvas,
45 x 100 cm.

Claude Monet,
The Boat, 1887,
oil on canvas,
146 x 133 cm.

Right:
Claude Monet,
Promenade Near
Argenteuil, 1873,
oil on canvas,
60 x 81 cm.

The fields of flowers in *Promenade*, filled with atmospheric notations and vibrating brushstrokes, radiate a triumphant Impressionism. This was one of Monet's favorite themes: fourteen years later, large groups of wild irises became pure chromatic studies. The mauve and yellow divisionist style demonstrates that the painter was concerned with the neo-Impressionist style that had just appeared. And his anxiety about a necessary artistic renewal underlies the moonlit boat floating in the current, weighted down with winding grasses. Returning to this project in 1890, Monet confided in Geffroy that he was attempting "impossible things: water with grass waving under the surface. It is crazy to want to do this."

TRAINS AND STATIONS

Subtle, intangible phenomena such as snow flurries and spiraling curls of smoke always fascinated Monet. *Train in the Snow* depicts the train he took, rain or shine, that ran just a few steps from his second house in Argenteuil. *The Pont de Europe* belonged to the series of Parisian stations, which contained the railway monsters described by Emile Zola. Eight paintings were included in the third Impressionist exhibition; Dr. de Bellio purchased this version. Portraits by Monet are more unusual. He used

Claude Monet,
Train in the Snow,
The Locomotive,
1875,
oil on canvas,
59 x 78 cm.

every shade of blue in the portrait by François Hippolyte Guillaume, known as Poly. Introduced by Australian painter John Russell, who lived on Belle-Isle, this fisherman from Kervilahouen showed Monet the wildest parts of the coastline in 1886. Although the artist exhibited this superb image several times, he never sold it.

Top to bottom:
Claude Monet,
Portrait of Poly,
1886,
oil on canvas,
74 x 53 cm.

Claude Monet,
*The Pont de l'Europe,
Gare Saint-Lazare*,
1877,
oil on canvas,
64 x 81 cm.

Claude Monet,
*Rouen Cathedral,
Effects of Sunlight,
Sunset,* 1892,
oil on canvas,
100 x 65 cm.

THE ROUEN CATHEDRAL

Top to bottom:
Claude Monet,
*The Seine at
Port-Villez, Evening
Effects*, 1894,
oil on canvas,
52 x 92 cm.

Claude Monet,
*The Seine at
Port-Villez,
Pink Effects*, 1894,
oil on canvas,
52 x 92 cm.

Painted in March and April of 1892 and 1893 in a building located opposite the cathedral, this work was later finished at Giverny. Although dispersed in various collections, the 28 paintings of the *Rouen Cathedral* series represent an entirely novel experiment: the composition is characterized by an abhorrence of empty space and a pictorial material treated as thickly as mortar.
This ambitious project – "colossal work… enormous difficulties" – haunted Monet's dreams. "The cathedral fell on top of me; it seemed to be blue, or pink or yellow." Here the contrast between the shadows and the sunlight on the doors and the Albane tower depict the many effects of dispersed light. Pissarro, Renoir and Cézanne all admired this masterpiece, which was praised by Clémenceau in *The Révolution des cathédrales*. Monet offered an alternative vision to this confrontation with stone in his unfinished views of the Seine at Port-Villez, which appear to be polished mirrors under a gossamer mist.

LONDON FOG

Monet took refuge in London during the war of 1870. There, almost unknown, he painted Westminster Palace, the house of Parliament, from the Victoria Embankment. Thirty years later, rich and famous, he rivaled the work by Turner and Whistler in close to 100 paintings depicting the fog on the Thames. He concentrated on three different themes: *Parliament, Waterloo Bridge* and *Charing Cross Bridge*. Painted from the Saint Thomas Hospital, the parliament has fascinating effects of backlighting. Between the mauve sky and the golden-fringed waves of the river, rises the abstract shape of a ghostly monument with tapered vertical lines, and ultramarine blue striped with emerald green, as modern as any of Rimbaud's cities. *The Waterloo Bridge* was painted from a room in the Savoy Hotel. Some of the pastels reveal the concise design of preparatory sketches in which a few lines suffice to define the arches, the shadows and the swirling water.

Claude Monet,
London.
The Parliament,
Reflections
on the Thames,
1899-1901,
oil on canvas,
81 x 92 cm.

WATER LILIES

The *Water Lilies* in
the Marmottan collection
include several of the
numerous variations on
this theme painted
by Monet in the last
third of his life. Annoyed
with all the artists
who invaded Giverny to
paint his favorite
landscapes, copying his
style, he withdrew to his
own plastic universe
within an enclosed area.
It consisted of two
parallel worlds: the flower
garden and the water
garden. His request to
create a pond in the fields
of the Epte was sent
in 1893 to the *préfet*; in it,
he specified that it was to

Claude Monet,
Water Lilies,
1914-17,
oil on canvas,
130 x 150 cm.

be a "pleasure for the eyes," as well as "a decor to be painted." The public discovered Japanese-style gardens during the Universal Exhibitions of 1878 and 1889. The Japanese exhibition organized by Bing in 1886 gave artists the idea of using flowers as a single subject (resulting in Van Gogh's *Sunflowers* and the hydrangea in Montesqieu's poems) and of painting the plant life in ponds. "Can't you go study some aquatic plant?" Pissarro asked his son Georges. The flower chosen by Monet was one of the favorite motifs of

Claude Monet,
*Water Lilies, Evening
Effects*, 1897-98,
oil on canvas,
73 x 100 cm.

the Modern Style.
Nenuphars decorated Gallé
vases, brooches by the
jeweler Vever (a neighbor
of the painter in Vexin),
as well as the candelabras
cast by the Alice Monet's
brothers, the Raingo
family, who created crafted
bronzework. Monet
exhibited the *Water Lilies*
in 1900, but as early
as 1897 he had already
imagined using
the design as a wall decor.
"Juxtaposed, they would
form a room with a
horizon of water." This was
an indirect reply to his
friend Mallarmé, to whom
he was supposed to give
a drawing in 1887 for
La Gloire, in a collection that
also included the *White*

Claude Monet,
Water Lilies, 1903,
oil on canvas
73 x 92 cm.

Left to right:
Claude Monet,
Water Lilies,
1916-19,
oil on canvas,
200 x 180 cm.

Claude Monet,
*Water Lilies
and Agapanthus*,
1914-17,
oil on canvas,
initially
200 x 130 cm,
now 140 x 120 cm.

Nenuphar. "One of those magical closed nenuphars that suddenly enclosed a empty space of intact dreams within its white hollows." The same subject, even closer to the spirit of Mallarmé, reappeared in 1914. Elements and shapes seem to fuse, the grasses spread out like fans and the great snowy cumuli appear to burst from the water while the flowers are created from a cloud. In 1909 Monet exhibited a widely anticipated series called *Water Landscapes*. After diverting the Ru River, an arm of the Epte, the pond was enlarged and many new plants were added. They formed islands that looked like the floral

barges the painter had
seen and admired
in Holland. The water lilies
seem to drift in the
shadow of the ash, willows
and poplar. "These water
landscapes and
reflections have become an
obsession," confided
Monet to Gustave Geffroy
in 1908. He was
forced to stop painting
this theme due to various
natural events (a flood
in 1910, a cyclone
in 1912, which "destroyed
the willows I was
so proud of") and to
bereavement: Alice
died in 1911, followed by
his son Jean in January
of 1914. He was
fascinated and consoled
by returning to the

Claude Monet,
Water Lilies,
1916-19,
oil on canvas,
150 x 197 cm.

Claude Monet,
The Water Lily Pond,
1917-19,
oil on canvas,
130 x 120 cm.

water garden. The plants along the riverbank began to appear in his work, including the cerulean-blue agapanthus. The saturated colors and twisted branches of the willows were inspired from the Ballet Russes. "A restful, energetic whiteness" that appears between the pink and yellow water lilies, framed by the light branches, seems to come straight from *Afternoon of a Faun*. Later, he was hypnotized by the surface of the water itself, and painted circular movements that were in direct contradiction to the work by Cézanne and the Cubists. Monet painted his water lily pond until his death, creating large pieces that, under Clémenceau's influence, entered French museums. Like Chinese poet Tchen Sin Yeou, who wrote *The Garden in a Mustard Seed*, the water lily pond represented the entire universe to Monet.

Claude Monet,
Water Lilies,
1916-19,
oil on canvas,
130 x 152 cm.

THE JAPANESE BRIDGE

Left: Claude Monet,
*Japanese Bridge
(The Water
Lily Pond)*, 1918,
oil on canvas,
100 x 200 cm.

Right:
Claude Monet,
Weeping Willow,
1918-19,
oil on canvas,
100 x 120 cm.

Starting in 1895, Monet began to paint the Japanese footbridge over the pond, a theme he often depicted over the years. The first paintings were very realistic, but in time the bridge became more abstract. The old artist sat to the west of the bridge, facing the wisteria-covered arch, exploring the changes that occurred according to the time of day or the season. He painted this bridge with a stubborn determination that was strengthened by the threat of the cataracts that started to interfere with his vision in 1912. The russet, green and yellow tones in this version (1918) were applied as thickly as on the *Rouen Cathedral* series; it reflects the expressionist style characteristic of the last years of the painter's work. The series devoted to the *Willows* on the northern side of the pond was painted during the war years. In 1917, his friend Mirabeau, a journalist and gardening advisor, died. Debussy, who saw Mélisande's streaming hair in these

trailing branches, died
soon after. These branches
weave a curtain behind
the feminine curve of the
trunk, colored pink
by the light of the rising
sun. When Monet
left the pond, it was to
paint the lime trees
on the northwest side of
the garden. The rose- and

clematis-covered facade
appears beyond the rose
garden. This work was
painted several months
before he underwent an
eye operation; the
exaggerated contrasts, the
furiously entangled
reds and greens, and the
violent color annihilate
the concept of space. In

Claude Monet,
*Japanese Bridge
(The Water Lily Pond)*,
1918-24,
oil on canvas,
89 x 100 cm.

the fiery glow of the
sunset, the Japanese
bridge was reduced to little
more than a rendering
of the two arches,
for the same reasons.
Everything in this
last phase prefigures
the abstract expressionists
who recognized
Monet as their precursor.

Claude Monet,
*The House Viewed
from the Rose
Garden,* 1922-24,
oil on canvas,
81 x 93 cm.

WISTERIA, IRISES AND ROSES

Monet often focused on certain flowers. In his garden, where each and every plant was part of the overall plan. When he was asked to paint the water lily decorations in the Biron *hôtel,* he decided to add a frieze of purple and white wisteria; these were the same flowers that shaded the bridge and festooned the deck. Several years later, after suffering months of color distortions and undergoing three operations on his eye, he regained his sight. He then returned to painting irises, another characteristic flower of the 1900's. He was particularly fond of the Japanese varieties planted around the pond; the tapering leaves and butterfly-like flowers

Right:
Claude Monet,
*Yellow and
Purple Irises*,
1924-25,
oil on canvas,
106 x 155 cm.

Claude Monet,
Wisteria, 1919-20,
oil on canvas,
100 x 300 cm.

blurred the outline of the pond. As for roses, he preferred the simple shapes of the original eglantine, or sweet-briar. This plant had made a spectacular comeback after falling out of fashion for many years. "I spent all summer working with a new feeling of joy," he wrote to the painter Barbier in 1925. This cheerfulness is reflected in the arch of flowers and leaves painted like a cherry branch by Hokusai or an almond tree by Van Gogh. Like Elstir's roses (for which Proust drew his inspiration from Monet), it was "a fair likeness of a portrait of a rose," transposed into this interior garden that contained the art of creation before it appeared on the canvas. From Clémenceau to Paul Valéry and Bérénice, Aragon's heroine, every visitor marveled at the flowerbeds filled with a succession of changing colors "as if the garden was [constantly] repainted."

Claude Monet,
The Roses,
1925-26,
oil on canvas,
130 x 200 cm.

CAILLEBOTTE AND MORISOT

These paintings by Caillebotte – the most realistic of the Impressionists – given to Monet and kept in his room until his death, reflect the long friendship between the two artists. *Street in Paris. Rain*, an extremely sensitive study for the painting in the Chicago

museum, represents the corner of the rue de Turin and rue de Moscou near the studio of their friend Manet. *The Piano Lesson* is one of many paintings on this theme, depicted in different styles by Degas, Manet, Renoir and Toulouse-Lautrec. *At the Ball*, one of Berthe Morisot's most classical paintings, was exhibited at the second Impressionist exhibition and purchased by Dr. de Bellio. One of the artist's friends, Puvis de Chavannes, may have helped with the sale, as he was a close friend of the princess Cantacuzène, who was related to the Romanian art collector.

Above:
Berthe Morisot
(1841-95),
At the Ball, 1875,
oil on canvas,
65 x 52 cm.

Center:
Gustave Caillebotte
(1848-94),
*Street in Paris,
Rain*, 1877,
oil on canvas,
54 x 65 cm.

Above: Gustave
Caillebotte,
The Piano Lesson,
1881, oil on canvas,
81 x 65 cm.

Paul Gauguin
(1848-1903),
Bouquet of Flowers,
1897,
oil on canvas,
73 x 93 cm.

GAUGUIN

This masterpiece in the Duhem collection, and one of the rare works by Gauguin from Tahiti in a French museum, illuminates the walls of the Marmottan. It was among the paintings sent in February 1897 to Daniel de Monfreid, a loyal friend who tried to sell the works. *Barbaric Stories, Delightful Days* and *The Dream* were also sent with this work, to which Gauguin added a word of advice: to store them "in hope for the day that they decide to pay me properly." The tablecloth and the mangoes reflect Gauguin's interest in Cézanne and the influence of Redon is visible in the transparency to the right. Yet the overall effect of this bowl, sculpted by the artist, reflects his own creative energy. From Tahiti he acquired his "fabulous colors, his sultry, yet filtered and silent ambiance," with which he created these flowers that lie somewhere between reality and imagination.

COROT, SISLEY AND GUILLAUMIN

Above:
Jean-Baptiste-Camille
Corot (1796-1875),
Pond of Ville-d'Avray
Seen Through
the Leaves, 1871,
oil on canvas,
43 x 55 cm.

by Constable in this work, an archetypal Impressionist image: the ephemeral blossoming of the fruit trees under the changing sky of the Ile-de-France. Monet, visiting the poet Maurice Rollinat in 1888, fell in love with the valley of the Creuse. Starting in 1893, Guillaumin came every year. The village of Crozant, the Genetin dam and the gleaming Auvergne autumns all contributed to his development toward expressionism.

Corot prefigured Impressionism, Sisley incarnated the movement and Guillaumin concluded it. Corot, who took refuge in Douai during the Commune, sold this painting to Duhem's uncle. This misty view of the pond close to his country home hangs on the walls of the Marmottan next to works by the Impressionists, who always admired this painter, and near the painting by Berthe Morisot, his student. Sisley, who was extremely sensitive to Corot, was also influenced

Top to bottom:
Alfred Sisley (1839-99), *Spring in the Environs of Paris, Apple Trees in Bloom*, 1879, oil on canvas, 45 x 61 cm.

Armand Guillaumin (1841-1927), *The Creuse at Genetin*, c. 1900, oil on canvas, 65 x 80 cm.

AT THE SEASIDE

The sea and its beaches have been preponderant themes in art since the Second Empire. Boudin, an Impressionist before his time, taught Monet his pictorial techniques. He devoted his life to depicting the visual effects of wind, mist, sails and summer strollers in Sainte-Adresse, Trouville and Honfleur. This is where Baudelaire, in 1859, stood in admiration before several hundred pastel studies "sketched from clouds, the most insubstantial and difficult subject to grasp in terms of form and color." The post-Impressionist generation was also influenced by these works. But the fragmented brushstrokes of Le Sidaner belie the apparent simplicity by creating a underlying mystery, while the linear and modulated definition by Lebasque, a friend of Bonnard and Matisse, reflects a tranquil life of pleasure.

RENOIR

Top to bottom:
Edouard Manet
(1832-83),
*Head of a Man
(Claude Monet),*
1874, India ink
wash, 17 x 14 cm.

Auguste Renoir
(1841-1919),
*Seated Young Girl
With White Hat,*
1884, pastel,
62 x 47 cm.

Above: Auguste
Renoir, *Portrait
of Mademoiselle
Victorine
de Bellio,* 1892,
oil on canvas,
55 x 46 cm.

These three portraits by Renoir all have distinctive characteristics: the somewhat stiff elegance of the future donor, the impertinent boredom of the professional model and the inner tension in the beautiful Camille Monet. In the latest portrait, that of Victorine de Bellio, the artist returned to a more flexible style after a severe Ingres-like period. His skillful use of pastel is clear in this red-haired young girl, an illustration of his favorite theme, adolescence. The portrait of Camille Doncieux, Monet's first wife, was painted during the great period at Argenteuil. It is bathed in the blue shadows that were so highly criticized at the time. The bequest from Michel Monet, born several months before the death of his mother, gives Camille a place of honor among the painters she so often welcomed in her home. Her beauty was enchanting at the time and even today, she still fascinates visitors to the Marmottan Museum.

Above: Auguste Renoir, *Portrait of Madame Claude Monet*, 1872, oil on canvas, 61 x 50 cm.

Left to right:
French school,
Jean Bourdichon
(c. 1475-1521),
The Kiss of Judas,
miniature
on parchment,
20 x 13.5 cm.

Southern French
(or Catalan) school,
The Crucifixion,
c. 1215, miniature
on parchment
from a psalm book,
16.7 x 11.8 cm.

Collection of Illuminations

by Caroline Lesage

"If you would like to learn about and love art, go see the great masters as often as you possibly can. When you can finally feel them, touch them with your spirit, savor their colors again and again, then you will start to understand." This was how Georges Wildenstein (1892-1963), one of the most famous art dealers of our century, explained his passion for art. Early on, he was taken to art galleries and major European museums by his father, Nathan Wildenstein, who was also a dealer for such collectors as Gulbenkian, Rothschild and David-Weill. For his fourteenth birthday he received two illuminated pages from a fifteenth-century manuscript and four years later, in 1910, he purchased a thirteenth-century *Crucifixion* from Maggs, a large London bookstore. This was the beginning of a collection that "Monsieur Georges," as he was called at Drouot, built up for more than 50 years.

In the eighteenth century most of the miniatures, which were highly prized by collectors, were torn from psalm books, books of hours, missals, antiphonaries and so on. The Wildenstein collection, which does not include any entire works, is representative of this period when books were cut up. Examples include a complete page removed from the *Hours of Etienne Chevalier* – the Chantilly Museum has magnificent fragments of this same book – and a miniature by Jean Perréal, *Alchemy* (stolen from the Saint Geneviève Library in 1850). Following the advice of Bernard Berenson and Charles Sterling, Georges Wildenstein created an exceptional collection that includes more than 300 medieval and Renaissance illuminated pages; the French and Italian schools are particularly well represented.

In 1971 his son, Daniel Wildenstein, was elected to the Académie des Beaux-Arts. He then offered his father's collection to the Institut de France and in 1980 presided over its installation in the Marmottan Museum, which hung the works exactly as they had been displayed in his father's office on the Rue de la Boétie.

FRENCH SCHOOL

Left to right:
Jean Fouquet
(c. 1420-77/81),
*Episode in the Life of
Vrain*, (exorcizing in
Notre-Dame de Paris),
miniature on
parchment from
the *Book of Hours of
Etienne Chevalier*,
22 x 14 cm.

French school,
1491-93, *The
Amiral de Gravile
Hunting Wild Boar*,
miniature on
parchment, page
from the *Terrier of
Marcoussis* created
for Louis Malet,
lord of Graville and
admiral of France,
37.6 x 27 cm.

Jean Perréal
(1455-1530),
Alchemy, the only
miniature
illustrating the poem
written in 1516
by Jean Perréal:
*Nature's Lament
to the Wandering
Alchemist*,
18.1 x 13.4 cm.

These three illuminations from the French school illustrated fifteenth- and sixteenth- manuscripts. Books of hours, popular in the fifteenth century among wealthy families, were collections of pious texts and prayers that were recited at canonical hours of the day. They were often elaborately decorated, like this page from the *Hours of Etienne Chevalier*, in which Jean Fouquet created a composition in perspective, the first of its kind in France. The "Terriers" on the other hand, were detailed inventories of a lord's property with a list of the taxes due by the inhabitants; these were used by the nobility. They are precious records of life in a domain, and often express the naturalistic style of the fifteenth century, as, for example, in this *Wild Boar Hunt*. Finally, *Alchemy*, a miniature by Jean Perréal, depicts the lesson given by Nature (a nude and crowned winged woman) to the alchemist, who represents the humanism of the Renaissance: the philosopher's stone must be *opus nature* and not *opus mecanice*.

ITALIAN SCHOOL

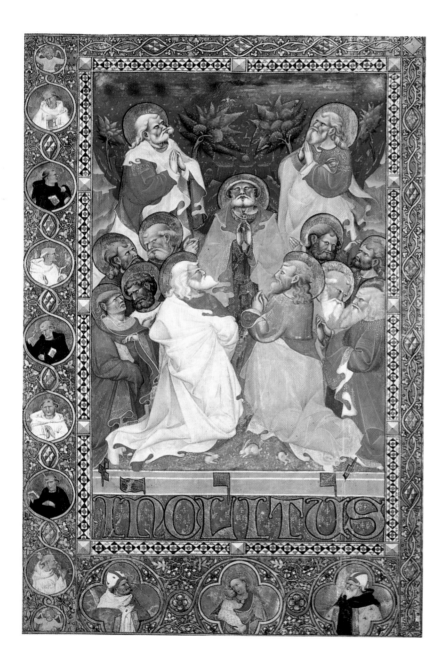

Left to right:
Lucchino di
Giovanni Belbello
da Pavia
(active c. 1430-62),
Lombardy,
*The Mission of the
Apostles*, miniature
on parchment,
54 x 36.5 cm.

Girolamo di
Giovanni dei Corradi
da Cremona (active
between 1451 and
1483), Lombardy, *The
Baptism of Constantin*,
1451, miniature
on parchment from
an antiphonary,
56 x 43 cm.

In fifteenth- and
sixteenth-century Italy, the
art of illumination
borrowed the forms and
new pictorial vocabulary
of the Renaissance.
The Mission of the Apostles
is still essentially
Byzantine and Gothic in
style; only the
playful rabbits seem to
be free from the
static composition.
In *The Baptism of
Constantin*, a page from a
collection of songs,
there is a balance in the
proportions between
the figures and the space
containing them,
while the scene offers
a perspective
toward the outside.

It is an extremely symbolic work, because the baptism of the Roman Emperor Constantin by Pope Sylvestre made Christianity the religion of the Empire. The superb ornamental capital letter, which consists of elements of classical architecture, prefigures the richly decorated margins of animals, foliated script, *putti* and architectural designs of the Italian Renaissance. The border around *The Dream of Saint Romuald* is a tentative example of this development.

Above: Attavante
(c. 1452-c.1525),
Florence, *The Dream
of Saint Romuald*,
c. 1502, miniature
on parchment,
44 x 34 cm.

Musée Marmottan
2, rue Louis Boilly 75016 Paris
Tél. : 01 42 24 07 02.
Fax : 01 40 50 65 84.

Ouvert toute l'année,
de 10h à 17h30, sauf le lundi.
Visites commentées sur demande.
Librairie-boutique.

Président-directeur général :
Charles-Henri Flammarion.
Directeur de la publication :
Jean-Christophe Delpierre.
Directeur de la rédaction : Nicolas Chaudun.
Secrétaire générale de la rédaction :
Pascale Bertrand.
Maquette : Claire Luxey,
sur un concept de Ruedi Baur.
Iconographie : Caroline Lesage,
assistée de Carol Chabert.
Secrétariat de rédaction : Isabelle Arson.
Version anglaise : Lisa Davidson.
Secrétariat de rédaction
pour la version anglaise : Isabelle Gilloots.
Directeur de la fabrication :
Alain Alliez, assisté de Nathalie Laudat.
Responsable des ventes : Isabelle Canals
Tél. : 01 45 38 30 60, fax : 01 45 38 30 61.

Beaux Arts S. A., 33, avenue du Maine,
75755 Paris Cedex 15.
Tél. : 01 45 38 30 00, fax : 01 45 38 30 01.
RCS Paris B 404 332 942.
Commission paritaire 65094.
Imprimé en Italie par Mariogros S.p.a., Turin.
Dépôt légal : avril 1997.

© Beaux Arts S. A.
Toutes photos Alban Couturier
sauf mention contraire.

Nous remercions pour l'aide qu'ils ont
apportée à la réalisation de cet ouvrage
M. d'Hauterives, Mme Delafond
et Mme Genêt, Mlle Fallek à la fondation
Wildenstein, ainsi que M. Peuchot,
directeur des services administratifs
de l'Institut de France.